Wish for a Candy Bar and Pizza

Wish for a Candy Bar and Pizza:

Poems for Kids

Written by Sarah Feola
Illustrations by Trey Feola

Prepared for publishing by Island Holiday Publishing
East Greenbush, NY

Wish for a Candy Bar and Pizza: Poems for Kids

First Edition
ISBN: 9798327787599

Cover colorization and design by Connie Fitsik from Island Holiday Publishing, featuring artwork by Trey Feola
Interior illustrations by Trey Feola

For My Babies.

TROUBLE

I'm in trouble
Not sure what I did
Banished to my room
I hate being a kid

Could it be I broke a vase
Could it be I pinched my sis
Could it be I tracked in mud
Yup, I did all of this

Mom and Dad are mad
They told me not to touch
They said "hands to yourself"
I didn't know dirt could stain so much

Next time I will listen
They only want what's best
But I wouldn't be a little kid
If I didn't put them to the test

DREAMLAND

Unicorns
Ogres
Fairies
And goons
Mom says if I hurry and go to sleep
I can dream of them soon

Far-away places
Colors galore
Don't wake me up yet
Let me dream some more

In the morning I will tell you
About my adventures and fun
Every detail
Every thing
Then tomorrow another one

NEW BABY

Baby…
What?
Poop…
Gross!
Spit Up…
Yuck!
Share…
No way!
Instant playmate…
OKAY!

IT

It's under my bed
I'm not going to look
It's under my bed
It has a hand that's a hook

It'll grab my toes
It'll tickle my feet
It'll take my toys
It'll steal all my treats

Okay – I’m looking
(okay – I’m a little scared)
What if it’s big
Bug-eyed and wire haired

Wait – I see nothing
No “it” under my bed
A sigh of relief, a chuckle
“It” was all in my head

MY BABY BOY

You are my baby boy
How I love you so
Just how much I love you
Is more than you can know

Your smiles make me happy
Your tears make me sad
Your hugs and kisses are the best
The best I've ever had

My love for you grows and grows
Never will it end
Good boy or naughty boy
My love won't break or bend

Always so dear
You are my sunshine
My baby boy
The special love of mine

GETTING READY

Brush my teeth…ugh
Brush my hair…ugh
Wash my face…ugh
Get dressed…ugh

Wait…I look great!

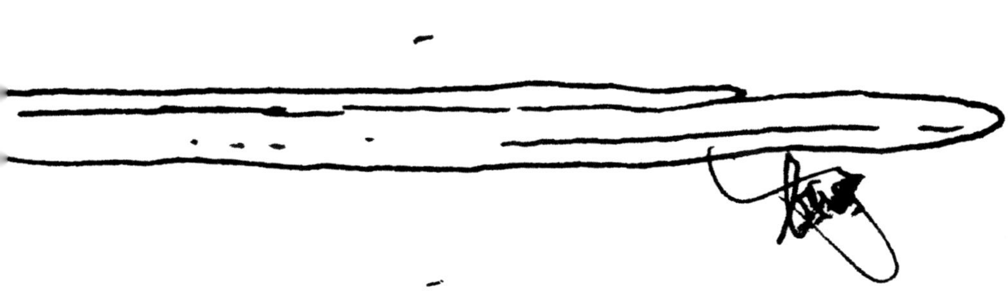

GOODNIGHT

Tell me a story Mama
Something wonderful and new
Tell me a story Mama
People, places, all made up by you

It helps me go to sleep
It helps shape my dreams
I listen to every word
(As sleepy as I seem)

When I have children
I will tell them stories too
Then watch them sleep sweetly
And Mama, I will think of you

MOMMY

Mommy...

Mommy...

Mommy...

Mommy...

Mommy!!!

Mommy!!

MY LITTLE BROTHER

My little brother
Always a mess
Dirty, dirty, yuck
But he couldn't care less

Leaving a trail
Wherever he goes
Socks here, toys there
Even yucky tissues from his nose

Paint on his pants
Food in his hair
He really needs a bath
Give him one if you dare

He may be weird
Crazy and such
But he's my little brother
And I love him so much

FLOWERS

Daffodil, Daisy, your colors all aglow
In the light of the sun, your radiance does show

Beautiful creations, Tulip, Mum, and Rose
Beautiful scents, magic to my nose

Tip-toeing through, or picking for my love
Making people happy, little gifts from above.

ALPHABET FEELINGS

Amazed
Bewildered
Confident
Delighted
Envious
Funny
Goofy
Happy
Impatient!
Jumpy
Kooky
Lazy
Mad
Nutty
Out of Control!
Proud
Queasy
Radiant
Sad
Tired
Unafraid
Vibrant
Weary
eXtraordinary
Yucky
Zealous

SUN AND MOON

I see the sun
I see the moon
One at midnight
One at noon

So far away
Up so high
So very beautiful
Up in the sky

Natural light
Guiding my way
So amazing
Both night and day

FOREVER FRIEND

I love my dog
And he loves me

After a long day
It's me he's happy to see

We run and play
We snuggle tight

He's my buddy and I am his
Our friendship is just right

SIBLINGS

Get away from me!

I don't like you.

You are gross!

I'm telling.

You're mean.

Leave me alone!

Stop bothering me!

I need your help.

Thank you.

That was nice.

I love you.

GROSS
I LOVE YOU

GRAPEVINE

I heard it through what
I heard it through who
I heard it through the grapevine
And now I'm telling you

It may not be true
It probably is wrong
I shouldn't spread a rumor
The truth from it is gone

I WANNA

I wanna play outside
I wanna play in the sun
I wanna ride my bike
I wanna have some fun
I wanna build a fort
I wanna make a mud pie
I wanna take a swim
I wanna watch my kite fly
I wanna play tag
I wanna seek and hide
I wanna watch the clouds
I DON'T WANNA STAY INSIDE!!!

You Look
Pretty

TAG

Tag,
You're it
Time to do something nice
Make someone's day
A compliment or simple smile would suffice

Tell someone they look pretty
Help complete a chore
Give someone a high-five
Even hold open a door

Then tag someone else
Tell them the game
Pass on the niceness
Have them do the same

BABY GIRL

You are my sun and moon
You are my stars so bright
You light up my days
You put the twinkle in my night

You are my baby girl
True love you have shown
Such an amazing gift
Nothing like I've known

M

WHEN I GROW UP

What do you want to be when you grow up?

A Cowboy?
A Princess?
A Doctor?
An Astronaut?
A Teacher?
A Farmer?
An Artist?

When I grow up, I want to be me...

...Good choice.

BUG

Bug, stop bugging me
You buzz by my ear
I feel you on my skin
I know you are flying near

I try to swat you away
I try to shoo you too
You follow me around outside
I go inside and you follow me on through

You need to go back out
You need to buzz away
You need to bug someone else
Enough bugging me today

I go to the window
Follow me you do
Off you go to bug another
You finally got my clue

Ribbit
Ribbit
Ribbit

NATURE'S LITTLE HOPPER

Little frog
Jumping all day
Here to there, there to here
Going wherever you may

Enjoying water, exploring land
A little bit of it all
No lake too deep
No tree too tall

May you stay happy
May you stay free
Nature's little hopper
Forever may you be

GROWTH

Egg (cool)
Larva (wow)
Pupa (awesome)
Butterfly (beautiful)

SUGAR RUSH

Up, down, here, there
Sit, stand, crawl
Sing, laugh, scream, cry
Sugar bounces me off the wall

I ate the candy
I ate the gum
And some ice cream
Now I can't stay mum

My belly hurts
I can't sit still
Too much sugar
Has made me ill

Mom said only a little
I must have had a lot
Boy, do I regret it
Cause sick is all I got

LOST

I have a loose tooth
Wiggle, wiggle, wiggle
Mom says to leave it alone
And watch what I eat

Mmm… a yummy apple…

NO MORE LOOSE TOOTH!

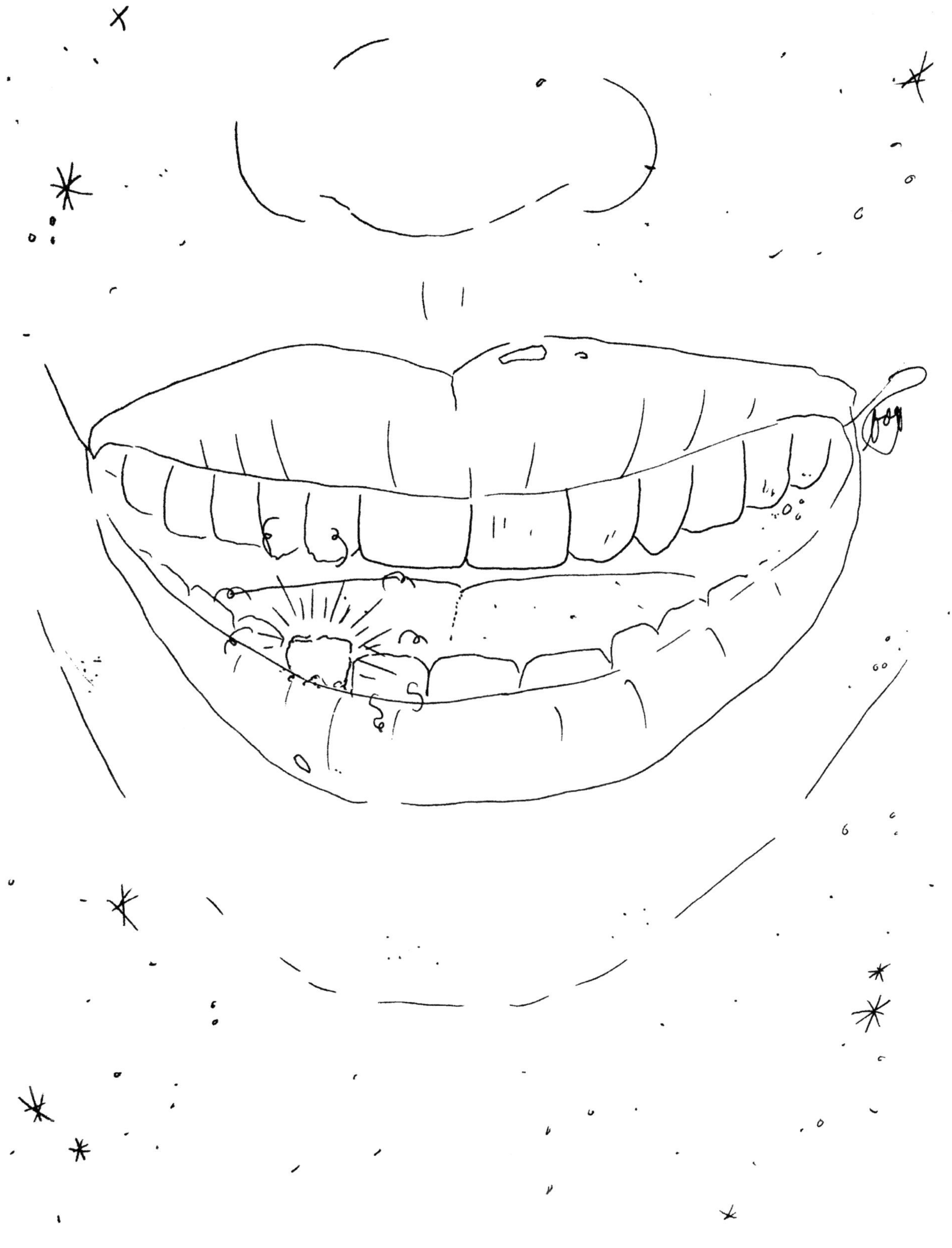

TORNADO TREY

Like a whirly twirly storm Trey comes through the room
He runs and jumps, yells and screams, hold on to your fork and spoon

Never mind the cleaning, it will just end up a mess
Do not bother ironing, he will only wrinkle your dress

Some peace and quiet, that would be nice
Loud singing, heavy stomping will just have to suffice

Shh... baby sister has to go to sleep
So stop pretending you are a car horn, beep beep beep

Time for bed, you must calm down
You silly boy, Mommy's little clown

A kiss goodnight, a tight hug too
There is no little boy I love more than you!

NIGHT WISH

Goodnight.
Love you.
Wish for a candy bar and pizza.

Made in the USA
Middletown, DE
06 December 2024

66276675R00033